COSMOS QUESTIONS
WHERE DO BLACK HOLES GO?

by Clara MacCarald

pogo

Ideas for Parents and Teachers

Pogo Books let children practice reading informational text while introducing them to nonfiction features such as headings, labels, sidebars, maps, and diagrams, as well as a table of contents, glossary, and index.

Carefully leveled text with a strong photo match offers early fluent readers the support they need to succeed.

Before Reading

- "Walk" through the book and point out the various nonfiction features. Ask the student what purpose each feature serves.
- Look at the glossary together. Read and discuss the words.

During Reading

- Have the child read the book independently.
- Invite them to list questions that arise from reading.

After Reading

- Discuss the child's questions. Talk about how they might find answers to those questions.
- Prompt the child to think more. Ask: Did you know about black holes before reading this book? What more would you like to learn about them?

Pogo Books are published by Jump!
5357 Penn Avenue South
Minneapolis, MN 55419
www.jumplibrary.com

Copyright © 2026 Jump! International copyright reserved in all countries. No part of this book may be reproduced in any form without written permission from the publisher.

Jump! is a division of FlutterBee Education Group.

Library of Congress Cataloging-in-Publication Data

Names: MacCarald, Clara, 1979- author.
Title: Where do black holes go? / by Clara MacCarald.
Description: Minneapolis, MN: Jump!, Inc., [2026]
Series: Cosmos questions | Includes index.
Audience: Ages 7–10
Identifiers: LCCN 2024059919 (print)
LCCN 2024059920 (ebook)
ISBN 9798892138642 (hardcover)
ISBN 9798892138659 (paperback)
ISBN 9798892138666 (ebook)
Subjects: LCSH: Black holes (Astronomy) –Juvenile literature.
Classification: LCC QB843.B55 M33 2026 (print)
LCC QB843.B55 (ebook)
DDC 523.8/875—dc23/eng/20250102
LC record available at https://lccn.loc.gov/2024059919
LC ebook record available at https://lccn.loc.gov/2024059920

Editor: Alyssa Sorenson
Designer: Emma Almgren-Bersie

Photo Credits: buradaki/Shutterstock, cover, 11 (background); Mohd. Afuza/Shutterstock, 1; Nazarii_Neshcherenskyi/Shutterstock, 3; JPL-Caltech/NASA, 4, 11 (foreground); EHT Collaboration, 4 (inset); muratart/Shutterstock, 5; TVEN/Shutterstock, 6-7; Elen/Alamy, 8-9; remotevfx/Shutterstock, 10; MARK GARLICK/SCIENCE PHOTO LIBRARY/Getty, 12-13; imagophotodesign/Shutterstock, 14-15; VICTOR de SCHWANBERG/Science Source, 16-17; Stocklekkies/Shutterstock, 18; Dabarti CGI/Shutterstock, 19; NASA, ESA, and D. Coe, J. Anderson, and R. van der Marel (STScI), 20-21; lembergvector/Adobe Stock, 23.

Printed in the United States of America at Corporate Graphics in North Mankato, Minnesota.

TABLE OF CONTENTS

CHAPTER 1
Dark and Dense....................................4

CHAPTER 2
Beyond Black Holes.............................10

CHAPTER 3
Life Cycle of Black Holes....................18

ACTIVITIES & TOOLS
Try This!..22
Glossary..23
Index...24
To Learn More....................................24

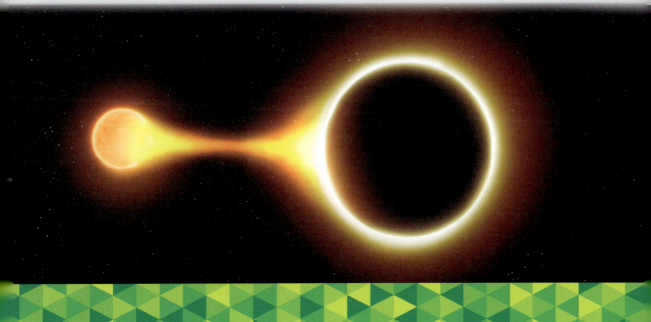

CHAPTER 1
DARK AND DENSE

A giant space object is in the center of our **galaxy**. It is 4.3 million times heavier than the Sun. It is a supermassive black hole! It is called Sagittarius A*.

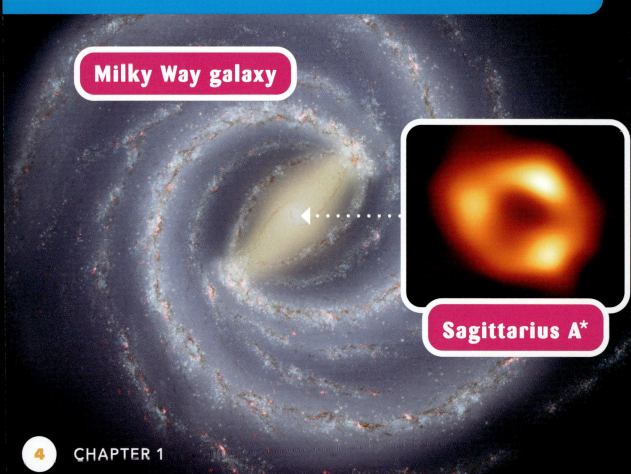

Milky Way galaxy

Sagittarius A*

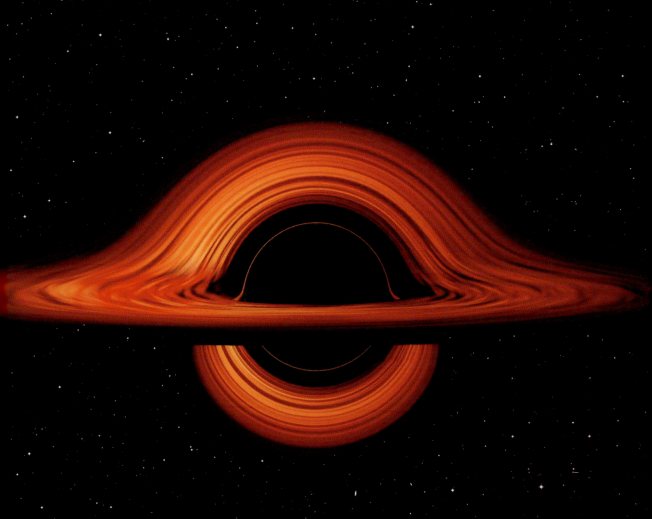

Black holes are not true holes. Instead, they are very **dense** objects. A huge amount of **matter** is packed into them. The **universe** has countless black holes. But we cannot see them.

CHAPTER 1 5

Black holes do not give off light. How do scientists find them? A black hole's **gravity** is very strong. It makes nearby stars **orbit** the black hole. It looks like the stars are orbiting nothing. It is a sign. A black hole may be there! A black hole's gravity pulls in gases, too. The gases swirl around the black hole. They get hot. They give off light.

DID YOU KNOW?

There are three types of black holes. Stellar-mass black holes are the smallest. Then there are intermediate-mass black holes. Supermassive black holes are the largest. They can be billions of times heavier than the Sun!

CHAPTER 1

CHAPTER 1

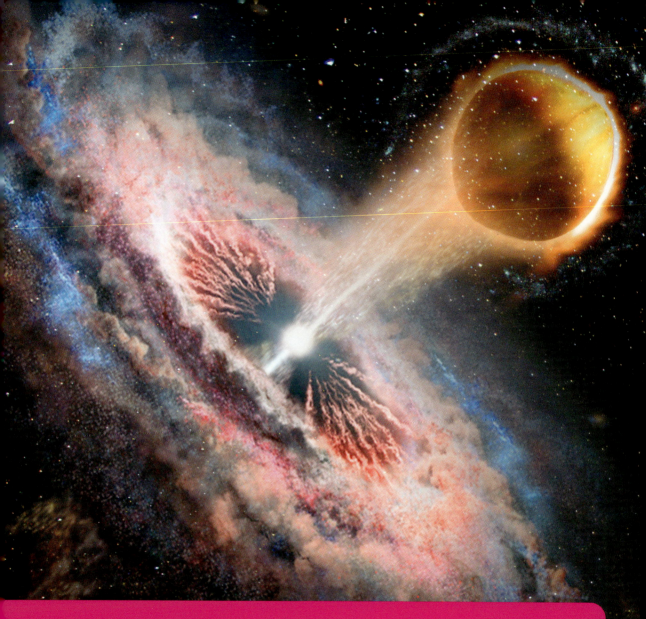

A black hole's gravity **captures** anything that gets too close. This includes gases, dust, planets, stars, and even light! A black hole **collects** matter. It grows.

CHAPTER 1

TAKE A LOOK!

Black holes come in all sizes. How big are some compared to the Sun? Take a look!

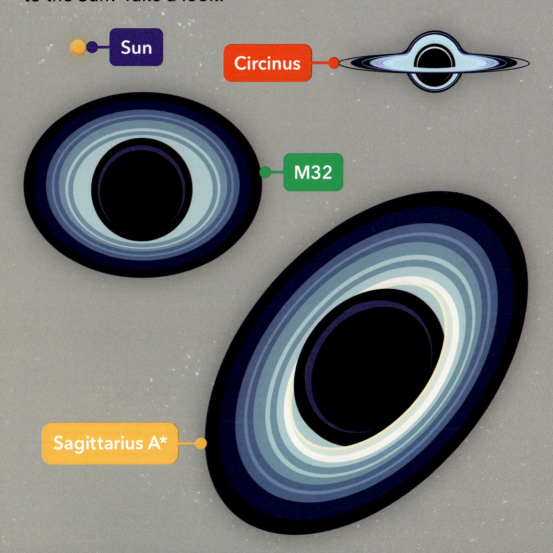

CHAPTER 1   9

CHAPTER 2
BEYOND BLACK HOLES

A black hole's surface is called the event horizon. Anything that enters the event horizon cannot escape. The gravity is too strong.

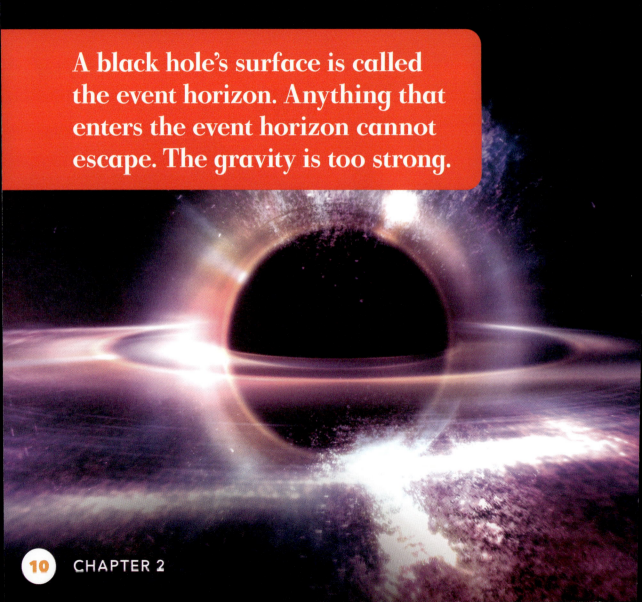

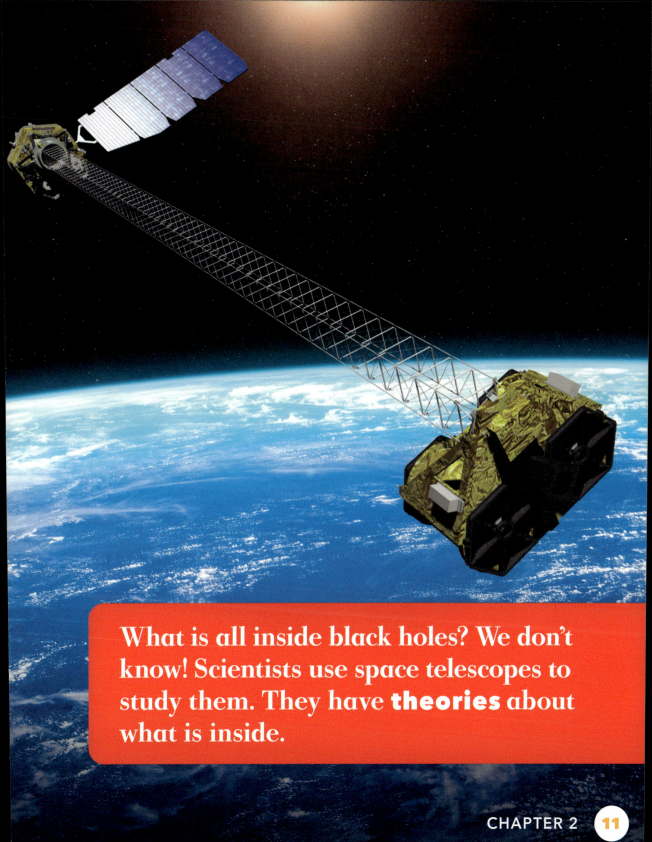

What is all inside black holes? We don't know! Scientists use space telescopes to study them. They have **theories** about what is inside.

CHAPTER 2 — 11

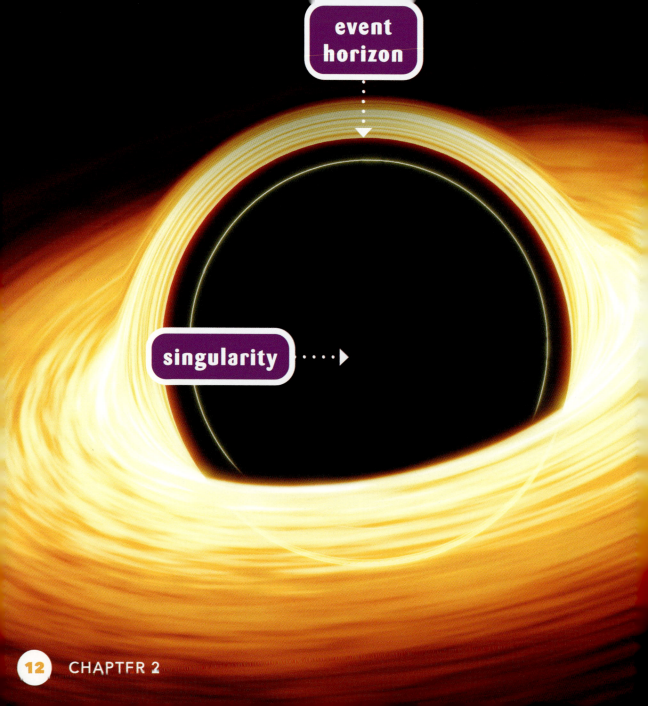

One theory has to do with the singularity. This may be a point at the center of a black hole. Things that pass the event horizon are torn apart. They may be added to the singularity. The more matter there is in the singularity, the bigger the event horizon gets.

DID YOU KNOW?

Some scientists don't believe in the singularity. Instead, they think a dense object is at the center of a black hole. They call it a Planck star. They think it could explode! Matter from the black hole would return to the universe.

Some people think each black hole has a tunnel. It is called a wormhole. It might lead to another part of space. It could even lead to another universe!

CHAPTER 2

CHAPTER 2

On the other side of the wormhole could be a white hole. A white hole is the opposite of a black hole. Everything can leave. But nothing new can enter. All the light shooting out would make it very bright!

Wormholes and white holes might not exist. Scientists keep looking for answers. They want to understand where black holes go.

DID YOU KNOW?

The universe likely began with a big bang. This is when everything shot out from one point. Some scientists wonder if that point was a white hole!

CHAPTER 2 17

CHAPTER 3

LIFE CYCLE OF BLACK HOLES

There are countless stars in our universe. Every star will eventually die. When massive stars die, they explode. A black hole may form as a result!

Galaxies move. Sometimes they run into each other. Black holes in the galaxies can crash together. They become one bigger black hole.

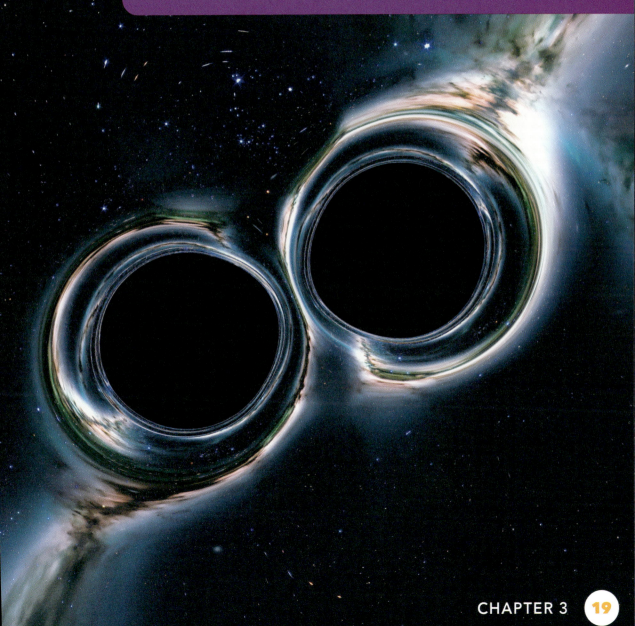

CHAPTER 3 | 19

Can a black hole die? Some scientists think so. Black holes may shrink over time. They might disappear. But it would take a very long time. How long? Longer than the universe has been around! So we may never know for sure.

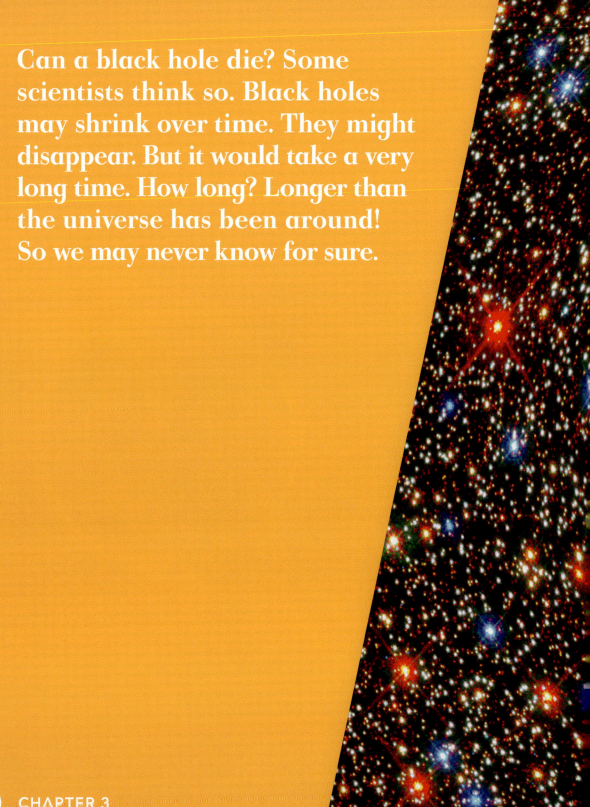

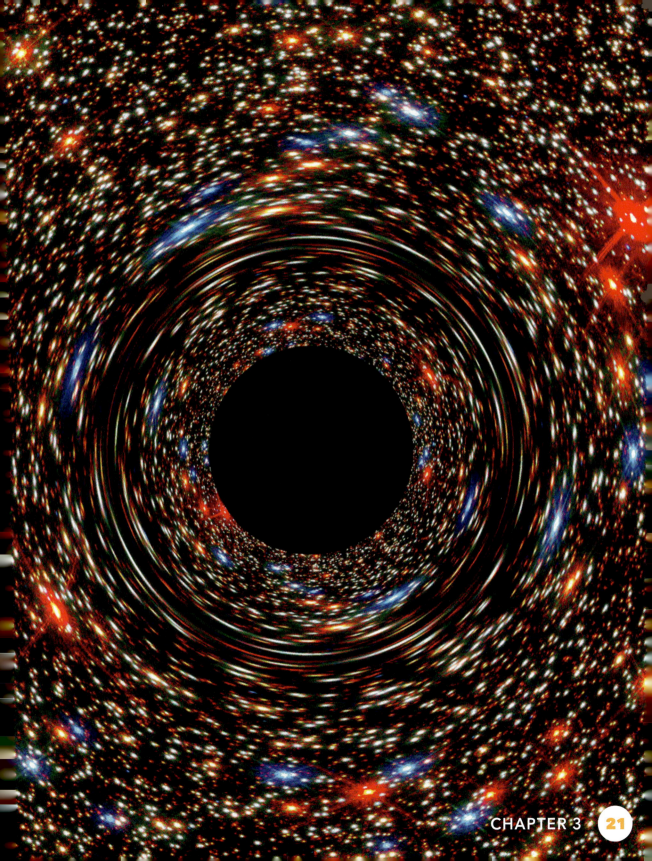

CHAPTER 3

ACTIVITIES & TOOLS

TRY THIS!

A MAGNETIC BLACK HOLE

How does a black hole work? Find out with this fun activity!

What You Need:
- magnet
- one small metal ball that sticks to the magnet

❶ Find the part on your magnet that the ball sticks to. Lay that side down, facing you. Make sure it is on a flat and clear area. The magnet is your black hole.

❷ The ball is a space object. Roll the ball toward the magnet. What happens?

❸ Roll the ball in different directions. What happens when you roll the ball closer to the magnet? What happens when you roll it farther away?

❹ How is a magnet like a black hole?

GLOSSARY

captures: Attracts and holds.

collects: Gathers things together.

dense: Packed together tightly.

galaxy: A very large group of stars and planets.

gravity: The force that pulls things toward the center of a space object and keeps them from floating away.

matter: Something that has weight and takes up space, such as a solid, liquid, or gas.

orbit: To travel in a circular path around something.

theories: Ideas based on some facts or evidence but not proved.

universe: All existing matter and space.

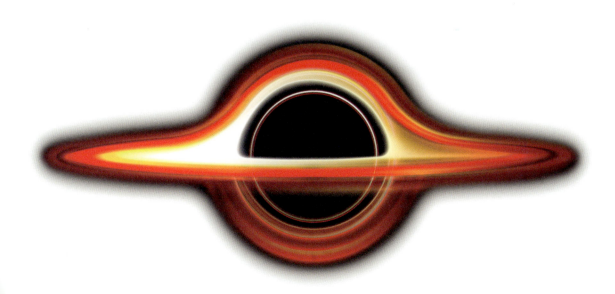

ACTIVITIES & TOOLS 23

INDEX

big bang 17
captures 8
Circinus 9
crash 19
dense 5, 13
event horizon 10, 13
explode 13, 18
galaxy 4, 19
gases 6, 8
gravity 6, 8, 10
light 6, 8, 17
matter 5, 8, 13

M32 9
orbit 6
Planck star 13
Sagittarius A* 4, 9
shrink 20
singularity 13
stars 6, 8, 13, 18
Sun 4, 6, 9
theories 11, 13
universe 5, 13, 14, 17, 18, 20
white hole 17
wormhole 14, 17

TO LEARN MORE

Finding more information is as easy as 1, 2, 3.

❶ Go to www.factsurfer.com
❷ Enter "blackholes" into the search box.
❸ Choose your book to see a list of websites.